JULIUS CAESAR

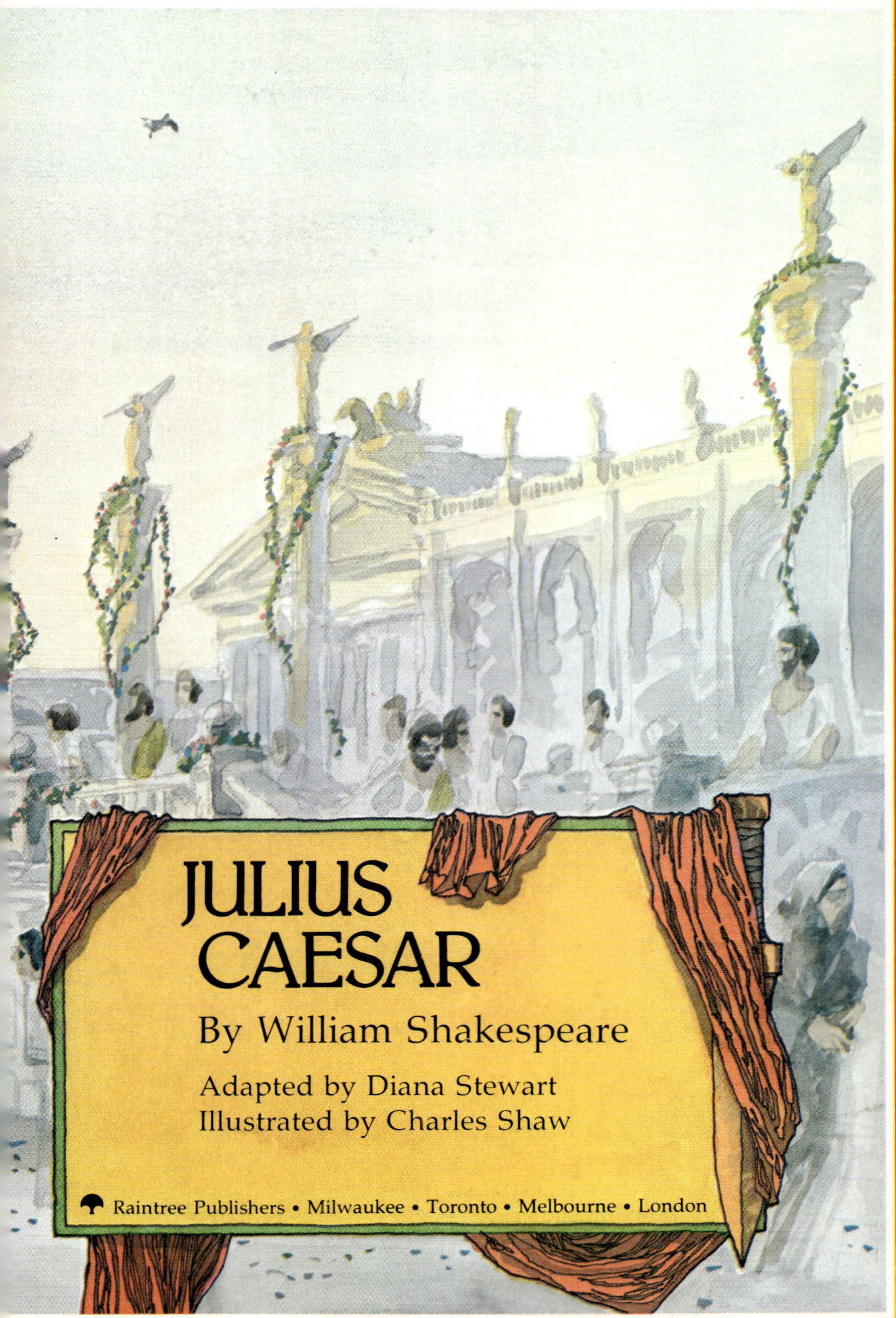

JULIUS CAESAR

By William Shakespeare

Adapted by Diana Stewart
Illustrated by Charles Shaw

Raintree Publishers • Milwaukee • Toronto • Melbourne • London

 Inquiries should be addressed to Raintree Publishers Inc., 205 West Highland Avenue, Milwaukee, Wisconsin 53203.
Library of Congress Number: 80-16406
3 4 5 6 7 8 9 0 84

Printed and bound in the United States of America.

Library of Congress Cataloging in Publication Data

Stewart, Diana.
Julius Caesar.

(Raintree short classics)
SUMMARY: Brutus, best friend of the Roman ruler Caesar, reluctantly joins a successful plot to murder Caesar and subsequently destroys himself.
1. Caesar, C. Julius — Juvenile drama. [1. Caesar, C. Julius — Drama. 2. Plays] I. Shakespeare, William, 1564-1616. Julius Caesar. II. Shaw, Charlie. III. Title. IV. Series.
PR2808.A25 1980 812'.54 80-16406
ISBN 0-8172-1664-2 (lib. bdg.)

CAST OF CHARACTERS

Julius Caesar – ruler of the Roman Empire
Mark Antony – a Roman nobleman and Caesar's dearest friend
Soothsayer – a prophet, seer
Calphurnia – Caesar's wife

THE CONSPIRATORS:
Brutus
Cassius
Casca
Trebonius
Decius
Metellus Cimber
Cinna

Portia – Brutus's wife
Artemidorus – a wise man of Rome
Titinius – Cassius's friend
Messala – Cassius's friend
Volumnius – Brutus's friend

SERVANTS TO BRUTUS:
Varro
Clitus
Claudius
Strato
Lucius

Pindarus – Cassius's servant

Various citizens, senators, and friends.

THE SETTING:

Most of the play takes place in Rome in 44 B.C. Later the action moves to the battlefields near Sardis and Philippi.

At the beginning of the play, the great and powerful Rome is ruled by Julius Caesar. Rome is a republic — with a Senate to help make the laws — but Caesar is becoming more and more powerful. Many of the Roman nobility are afraid that he will be crowned king. These Roman leaders are frightened that this would mean an end to their freedom.

ACT I

The scene is a street in Rome. Rome is celebrating Caesar's great victories in war. The entire city has been decorated for the celebration. People have gathered to see Caesar and watch the sports that have been planned.

Caesar enters. He is accompanied by Antony, his closest friend; Calphurnia, his wife; and other noble leaders of the republic — Decius, Cicero, Cassius, Casca, and Brutus.

A soothsayer — a prophet — stands waiting for him in the cheering crowd as he approaches.

SOOTHSAYER. Caesar!

CAESAR. Who is it in the crowd that calls on me?
I hear a tongue cry "Caesar!" Speak! Caesar
Is turned to hear.

SOOTHSAYER. Beware the ides of March.

CAESAR. (To his friends) What man is that?

BRUTUS. A soothsayer bids you beware the ides
of March.

CAESAR. Set him before me. Let me see his face.

(*Cassius beckons the prophet nearer.*)

CASSIUS. Fellow, come from the throng. Look
upon Caesar.

CAESAR. (To the soothsayer)
What say'st thou to me now?
Speak once again.

SOOTHSAYER. Beware the ides of March.

CAESAR. (Turning away from him) He is a dreamer.
Let us leave him. Pass.

(*Caesar and his friends — except for Brutus and Cassius — leave to watch the games. In the distance comes the sound of trumpets and a great shout.*)

BRUTUS. What means this shouting? I do fear the people
Choose Caesar for their king.

CASSIUS. Ay, do you fear it?
Then must I think you would not have it so.

BRUTUS. I would not, Cassius. Yet I love him well.

(*Cassius is the leader of a group of conspirators — men who are plotting to kill Caesar. Now he sees his chance to win Brutus to his cause.*)

CASSIUS. I know you for an honorable man, Brutus.
Well, honor is the subject of my story.
I cannot tell what you and other men
Think, but for myself, I am not in awe of Caesar.
I was born free as Caesar. So were you!
We both have fed as well, and we can both
Endure the winter's cold as well as he.

Once Caesar said to me, "Darest thou, Cassius,
Now leap in with me into this angry river
And swim to yonder side?" So I plunged in
And bade him follow. So indeed he did.

But before we could arrive at the point proposed,
Caesar cried: "Help me, Cassius, or I sink!"
So from the waves of the river
Did I carry the tired Caesar. And this man
Is now become a god, and Cassius is
A poor, unhappy creature, and must bow
If Caesar carelessly but nod at him!

(*Again from the distance comes the blare of trumpets and the shouting of the crowd.*)

BRUTUS. Another general shout?
I do believe that these applauses are
For some new honors that are heaped on Caesar.

CASSIUS. Why, man, he doth stand like a giant

And we little men walk under his huge legs
And look about at our cowards' graves.

Men at some time are master of their fates.
The fault, dear Brutus, is not in our stars,
But in ourselves, that we are underlings.

Brutus and Caesar! What is in the name Caesar?
Why should that name be sounded more than yours?
Write them together, yours is as fair a name.
Sound them. It doth become the mouth as well.
Weigh them. It is as heavy.

Now, in the names of all the gods at once,
Upon what meat doth this our Caesar feed
That he is grown so great?

BRUTUS. That you do love me, Cassius, I know.
What you would have me do, I have some idea.
But for the present, say no more, I beg you!

What you have said, I will consider.
What you have to say, I will hear with patience.
Till we meet again, my noble friend, consider this:
Brutus would rather be a slave
Than to call himself a son of Rome and
Live under a tyrant!

CASSIUS. I am glad
That my weak words have struck but thus much show
Of fire from Brutus.

BRUTUS. Caesar is returning.

CASSIUS. As they pass by, pluck Casca by the sleeve,
And he will tell you what hath happened today.

BRUTUS. I will do so.

(Caesar and Antony stop a little way away. Caesar looks over to where Brutus and Cassius stand watching.)

CAESAR. Antony.

ANTONY. Caesar?

CAESAR. Let me have men about me that are fat,
Sleek-headed men, and such as sleep at night.
Yond Cassius has a lean and hungry look.
He thinks too much. Such men are dangerous.

(*Caesar and Antony exit with their followers, but Brutus catches Casca by the cloak to stop him.*)

CASCA. (To Brutus) You pulled me by the cloak.
Would you speak to me?

BRUTUS. Ay, Casca. Tell us what hath happened today
That Caesar looks so serious.

CASCA. Why, there was a crown offered him. And
When he refused the crown, the people fell
to shouting.

BRUTUS. What was the second noise for?

CASCA. Why, for that too.

CASSIUS. They shouted thrice. What was the last cry for?

CASCA. Why, for that too.

CASSIUS. Who offered him the crown?

CASCA. Why, Antony.

BRUTUS. Was the crown offered him three times?

CASCA. Ay, it was. And three times he refused it.
But for all that — to my thinking — he would
Have gladly had it. When he refused it the
Third time, he fell down fainting!

CASSIUS. What? Did Caesar faint?

CASCA. (In disgust) He fell down in the market place, and foamed at the mouth, and was speechless. But when he saw the people were glad he refused the crown, he plucked open his coat and offered them his throat to cut. If I had been a man of worth, I would have taken him at his word! And so he fell.

BRUTUS. And after that, he came so thoughtful away?

CASCA. Ay.

(Casca's words have troubled Cassius. Caesar was growing more and more popular with the people. It would not be long now before Caesar accepted the crown and became king. Cassius needed to move more quickly with his plans to kill Caesar.)

CASSIUS. Will you sup with me tonight, Casca?

CASCA. No, I am already promised.

CASSIUS. Will you dine with me tomorrow?

CASCA. Ay, if I be alive, and your mind the same, and your dinner worth eating.

CASSIUS. Good! I will expect you.

CASCA. Do so. Farewell, both.

BRUTUS. What a blunt fellow is he grown to be.

CASSIUS. But bold when the work is noble.

BRUTUS. Cassius, for this time I will leave you.
Tomorrow, if you please to speak with me,
Come home to me, and I will wait for you.

CASSIUS. I will do so. Till then, think of what I have said.

ACT II

Scene 1

The scene is Brutus's house. It is very late the following night. A terrible storm rages outside.

Deep in thought, Brutus convinces himself that Caesar is a danger to Rome's liberty — for if he is crowned king, he might turn into a tyrant that no one can stop.

For a while Brutus watches the thunder and lightning outside. Then he calls a servant to him.

BRUTUS. Is not tomorrow, boy, the ides of March?

SERVANT. Sir, March is wasted fifteen days.

BRUTUS. 'Tis good. (A knock sounds at the door) Go to the gate. Somebody knocks.

BRUTUS. Since Cassius first did speak against Caesar,
I have not slept.

(*The servant returns.*)

SERVANT. Sir, 'tis Cassius at the door,
Who doth desire to see you.

BRUTUS. Is he alone?

SERVANT. No, sir. There are more with him.

BRUTUS. Do you know them?

SERVANT. No, sir. Their hats are pulled about their ears.
And half their faces are buried in their cloaks.

BRUTUS. Let them enter.

(*The servant leaves and returns with the conspirators: Cassius, Casca, Decius, Cinna, Metellus Cimber, and Trebonius.*)

CASSIUS. Good morrow, Brutus. Do we wake you?

BRUTUS. I have been up this hour, awake all night.
(*He looks closely at the other men.*)
Know I these men that come along with you?

CASSIUS. Yes, every man of them; and no man here
But honors you. And every one doth wish
You had but that opinion of yourself

Which every noble Roman has for you.

BRUTUS. They are all welcome.
Give me your hands all over, one by one.

CASSIUS. Together we swear an oath to free Rome
From this tyrant Caesar.

DECIUS. Shall no man else be touched but only Caesar?

CASSIUS. I think it is not wise that Mark Antony —
So well beloved of Caesar — should outlive Caesar.
He is dangerous. Let Antony and Caesar fall together.

BRUTUS. (Very upset at the idea of killing Antony also) Our course will seem too bloody, Cassius! Let's be the saviors of Rome — but not the butchers! We fight against tyranny. Alas Caesar must bleed for it! Noble friends, let's kill him boldly, but not in anger. Let's carve him as a dish fit for the gods, not hew him as a carcass fit for the hounds. We shall be called heroes, not murderers. And for Mark Antony, think not of him! For he can do no more than Caesar's arm when Caesar's head is off.

CASSIUS. Yet I fear him — for the love he bears to Caesar.

BRUTUS. Alas, good Cassius, do not think of him.

TREBONIUS. There is no danger in him. Let him not die,
For he will live and laugh at this hereafter.
(*The clock strikes the hour.*)

BRUTUS. Peace! Count the clock.

TREBONIUS. 'Tis time to part.

CASSIUS. But it is doubtful yet
Whether Caesar will come forth today or not.
He has grown superstitious of late.
The words of his soothsayers
May keep him from the Capitol today.

DECIUS. Never fear that. I will bring him to the Capitol.

CASSIUS. Nay, we will all of us be there to fetch him.

BRUTUS. By the eighth hour. Is that the latest?

CINNA. Be that the latest, and fail not then.

CASSIUS. The morning comes upon us. We'll leave you, Brutus.
And, friends, all remember what you have said,
And show yourselves true Romans.

BRUTUS. And so good morrow to you every one.

(They all depart, leaving Brutus alone with his unhappy thoughts. Portia — his wife — enters.)

PORTIA. Brutus, my lord.

BRUTUS. Portia, what mean you? Wherefore rise you now?

PORTIA. Brutus, you have unkindly stolen from my bed. And yesternight at supper you suddenly rose and walked about, musing and sighing. And when I asked you what the matter was, you stared upon me with ungentle looks. I urged you further. Yet you answered not, but gave sign for me to leave you. Dear, my lord, tell me the cause of your grief.

BRUTUS. I am not well in health, and that is all.

PORTIA. Is Brutus sick and is he wise to walk
In the dank morning air to add upon his sickness?
(*She kneels at his feet.*)
No, my Brutus. You have some sickness within your mind
Which by the right and virtue of my place
I ought to know of. And upon my knees
I beg you — by all your vows of love —
That you unfold to me, your self, your half,
Why you are so worried, and what men tonight
Came to you. For here have been
Some six or seven, who did hide their faces
Even from darkness.

BRUTUS. Kneel not, gentle Portia.

PORTIA. Within the bond of marriage, tell me, Brutus!

(*He helps her to her feet and holds her close.*)

BRUTUS. You are my true and honorable wife,
As dear to me as are the drops of red blood
That visit my sad heart.

PORTIA. If this were true, then tell me your secrets.
I will not disclose them.

BRUTUS. O ye gods! Render me worthy of this noble wife!
Portia, wait a while and by and by, thy bosom shall
Know the secrets of my heart.

Scene 2

The scene is Caesar's house in the early hours of the same morning. The thunder and lightning are still heard outside. Julius Caesar enters in his nightrobe.

CAESAR. Neither heaven nor earth have been at peace tonight.
Three times hath Calphurnia in her sleep cried out,
"Help, ho! They murder Caesar!"

(*He calls for a servant.*)

SERVANT. My lord?

CAESAR. Go bid the priests offer a sacrifice and
Tell me what they say will occur today.

(*The servant exits to do his bidding. Calphurnia comes in. She is upset that Caesar is up and getting ready to go to the Capitol.*)

CALPHURNIA. What mean you, Caesar? Think you to walk forth?
You shall not stir out of your house today!

CAESAR. Caesar shall go forth. The things that threaten me

Will vanish when they see the face of Caesar.

CALPHURNIA. Caesar, I never believed in omens.
Yet now they frighten me. Most horrid scenes
Have been seen by the nightwatchmen!

A lioness hath given birth in the streets
And the graves have yawned, and yielded up their dead.
Fierce fiery warriors fought upon the clouds.
Their blood drizzled upon the Capitol.
The noise of battle sounded in the air.
Horses did neigh and dying men did groan.
And ghosts did shriek and squeal about the streets.

O Caesar, these things are unnatural,
And I do fear them!

CAESAR. Yet Caesar shall go forth — for these signs
Are for the world in general, not for Caesar alone.

CALPHURNIA. When beggars die, there are no comets seen!
The heavens themselves blaze forth the death of princes.

CAESAR. Cowards die many times before their death;
The valiant never taste of death but once.
Of all the wonders that I yet have heard,
It seems to me most strange that men should fear,
Seeing that death, a necessary end,
Will come when it will come.

(The servant returns with the predictions of the soothsayers.)

CAESAR. What say the priests?

SERVANT. They would not have you stir forth today.
Plucking the insides of an offering forth,
They could not find a heart within the beast.

CALPHURNIA. (Pleading with Caesar) Alas, my lord,
Do not go forth today. Call it my fear

That keeps you in the house and not your own.
We'll send Mark Antony to the Senate House
And he shall say you are not well today.
Let me, upon my knee, prevail in this.

(*Calphurnia kneels before Caesar, and he cannot bear to see her so worried and unhappy.*)

CAESAR. For you, I will stay at home.

(*As Calphurnia rises, Decius enters to bring Caesar to the Capitol.*)

CAESAR. Here's Decius. He shall tell them so.

DECIUS. Caesar, all hail! Good morrow, worthy Caesar.
I come to fetch you to the Senate House.

CAESAR. And you are come in very happy time
To bear my greeting to the senators,
And tell them that I will not come today.

CALPHURNIA. Say he is sick.

CAESAR. Shall Caesar send a lie?
Decius, go tell them Caesar will not come.

DECIUS. Most mighty Caesar, let me know some cause,
Lest I be laughed at when I tell them so.

CAESAR. The cause is in my will. I will not come.
That is enough to satisfy the Senate!
But for your private satisfaction —
Because I love you — I will let you know.

Calphurnia here, my wife, keeps me at home.
She dreamt last night she saw my statue,
Which, like a fountain with a hundred spouts,
Did run pure blood, and many lusty Romans
Came smiling and did bathe their hands in it.

And these does she see as warnings and signs
Of evil nearby, and on her knee
Has begged that I will stay at home today.

DECIUS. This dream is wrongly interpreted.

It is a vision fair and fortunate.

Your statue spouting blood in many pipes —
In which so many smiling Romans bathed —
Shows that from you, great Rome shall suck
Life-giving blood, and that great men shall come
To honor you. This is what is meant by
Calphurnia's dream.

CAESAR. (Flattered by these words) And you have explained it well.

DECIUS. I have, when you have heard what I can say.
The Senate have decided to give this day a crown to
Mighty Caesar. If you shall send them word you will
Not come, their minds may be changed.

Someone may mock you and say,
"Break up the Senate till another time,
When Caesar's wife shall meet with better dreams."
If Caesar hides himself, shall they not whisper,
"Lo, Caesar is afraid?"

Pardon me, Caesar, my dear dear love for you
Bids me tell you this.

CAESAR. How foolish do your fears seem now, Calphurnia!
I am ashamed I did yield to them.
Give me my robe, for I will go.

Scene 3

Artemidorus — a wise man of Rome and a teacher — stands on the street near the Capitol. He holds the letter he has written to Caesar. He reads it aloud.

ARTEMIDORUS. "Caesar, beware of Brutus.
Take heed of Cassius. Come not near Casca. Have an eye to Cinna. Trust not Trebonius. Mark well Metellus

Cimber. Decius loves thee not. There is but one mind in all these men — and it is set against Caesar. If thou are not immortal, look about you. Safety gives way to danger and plotting. The mighty gods defend thee!

Thy devoted follower,
Artemidorus"

Here will I stand till Caesar pass along,
And as a friend will I give him this.
My heart cries that virtue cannot live
Without jealousy and envy.
If thou read this, O Caesar, thou mayest live;
If not, the Fates are on the side of traitors.

ACT III

Scene 1

The scene is the street in front of the Capitol. Caesar, Brutus, Cassius, Casca, Decius, Metellus Cimber, Trebonius, Cinna, Antony, Artemidorus, and the Soothsayer enter with a sound of trumpets.

CAESAR. (To the soothsayer) The ides of March are come.

SOOTHSAYER. Ay, Caesar, but not gone.

(Artemidorus hurries to Caesar to give him the letter of warning.)

ARTEMIDORUS. Hail, Caesar! Read this petition!

DECIUS. (Pushing Artemidorus out of the way)
Trebonius doth desire you to read his humble petition.

ARTEMIDORUS. O Caesar, read mine first; for mine's a suit

That touches Caesar nearer. Read it, great Caesar.

CAESAR. What touches us ourself shall be read last.

ARTEMIDORUS. Delay not, Caesar! Read it instantly!

DECIUS. (Pushing him farther away from Caesar) Out of the way, Sirrah!

(Caesar moves on to the steps of the Capitol. Cassius turns nervously to Casca and Brutus.)

CASSIUS. I fear our purpose is discovered!
We must act quickly! Look you, Brutus.
Trebonius draws Mark Antony out of the way.

(Antony and Trebonius exit. The men crowd around Caesar. With Antony out of the way, they are all his enemies. Casca raises his dagger and strikes Caesar first. The others soon follow. Brutus stabs him last of all.)

CAESAR. *Et tu, Brute?* Then fall Caesar.

(He falls and dies.)

CINNA. Liberty! Freedom! Tyranny is dead!
Run hence, proclaim, cry it about the streets!

CASSIUS. Cry out "Liberty and freedom!"

(Their cries have brought the senators and townspeople running. When they see Caesar's bloody corpse, they flee.)

BRUTUS. People, and senators, be not afraid.
Do not flee! Ambition's debt is paid.

(Trebonius enters.)

CASSIUS. (To Trebonius) Where is Antony?

TREBONIUS. Fled to his house.
Men, wives, and children stare, cry out and run,
As if it were doomsday.

BRUTUS. Stoop, Romans, stoop,
And let us bathe our hands in Caesar's blood
Up to the elbows, and besmear our swords.

Then walk we forth, even to the market place,
And waving our red weapons over our heads,
Let's all cry "Peace, freedom, and liberty!"

CASSIUS. Stoop then, and wash. How many ages yet to come
Shall hear of our act. We shall be called
The men that gave their country liberty.

(Antony's servant enters.)

BRUTUS. Wait! Who comes here? A friend of Antony's.

SERVANT. If Brutus will swear that Antony
May safely come to him and know
Why Caesar hath deserved to lie in death,
Mark Antony shall not love Caesar dead
So well as Brutus living.

BRUTUS. Thy master is a wise and valiant Roman.
I never thought him worse.
Tell him, so please him come unto this place,
He shall be satisfied and, by my honor,
Depart unharmed.

(The servant leaves to bring back Antony.)

BRUTUS. I know that we shall have him as a friend.

CASSIUS. I wish we may. But yet have I a mind
That fears him much.

(Antony enters.)

BRUTUS. But here comes Antony. Welcome, Mark Antony.

ANTONY. (Looking sadly at Caesar's bloody corpse)
O mighty Caesar! Dost thou lie so low?
Are all thy conquests, glories, triumphs, spoils,
Shrunk to this little measure? Fare thee well.

(To the conspirators)
I know not, gentlemen, what you intend,
Who else must die.

If I myself, there is no hour so fit
As Caesar's death's hour, nor no instrument
Of half that worth as those your swords, made rich
With the most noble blood of all this world.

BRUTUS. O Antony, beg not your death of us!
Though now we must appear bloody and cruel,
Our hearts you see not. We do receive you
With all kind love, good thoughts, and reverence.

Only be patient till we have satisfied
The people, beside themselves with fear —
And then we will tell you the cause
Why I, that did love Caesar when I struck him,
Have thus proceeded.

ANTONY. I doubt not your wisdom.
Let each man give me his bloody hand.

(*Antony shakes hands with each of the conspirators, and then he speaks more to himself than to them.*)

ANTONY. O Caesar! If thy spirit look upon us now,
Shall it not grieve thee worse than death
To see thy Antony making his peace,
Shaking the bloody fingers of thy foes
In the presence of thy corpse?
Pardon me Julius!

CASSIUS. Mark Antony, I blame you not for praising Caesar so.
But what compact mean you to have with us?
Will you be numbered among our friends?

ANTONY. Friends am I with you all, and love you all.
But pray, tell me reasons why Caesar was dangerous.

BRUTUS. Our reasons are so full of good cause,
That were you, Antony, the son of Caesar,
You should be satisfied.

ANTONY. That's all I seek.
And I also ask that I may bring his body
To the market place, and in the pulpit,

Speak at his funeral, as becomes a friend.

BRUTUS. You shall, Mark Antony.

(*Cassius pulls Brutus aside.*)

CASSIUS. Brutus, you know not what you do! Do not consent
That Antony speak in his funeral.
Know you how much the people may be moved
By that which he will say?

BRUTUS. Cassius, I will myself speak first,
And show the reason of our Caesar's death.

CASSIUS. I like it not!

(*Brutus turns back to Antony.*)

BRUTUS. Mark Antony. Here, take you Caesar's body.
You shall not in your funeral speech blame us,
But speak all good you can devise of Caesar.
And say you do it by our permission.

ANTONY. Be it so. I do desire no more.

BRUTUS. Prepare the body, then, and follow us.

(*The conspirators exit, leaving Antony alone.*)

ANTONY. (Speaking to Caesar's corpse)
O pardon me, that I am meek and gentle with these butchers!
Thou art the ruins of the noblest man that ever lived.
Woe to the hand that shed this costly blood.
Over thy wounds now do I prophesy.
A curse shall fall upon the limbs of men.
Fury and war shall reign over all parts of Italy.
Blood and destruction shall rule
And Caesar's spirit seek his revenge!

Scene 2

The scene is the market place. People have now gathered to hear why Caesar has been killed. Brutus and

Cassius enter, and Brutus goes to the pulpit to speak to the crowd.

BRUTUS. Romans, countrymen, and friends, hear me and be silent! Believe me for mine honor. Judge me in your wisdom.

If there be any in this assembly — any dear friend of Caesar's — to him I say that Brutus's love for Caesar was no less than his. If then that friend demand why Brutus rose against Caesar, this is my answer: Not that I loved Caesar less, but that I loved Rome more. Had you rather Caesar were living, and die all slaves, than that Caesar were dead, to live all free men?

As Caesar loved me, I weep for him. As he was fortunate, I rejoice at it. As he was valiant, I honor him. But as he was ambitious, I slew him. There are tears, for his love; joy, for his fortune; honor, for his valor; and death, for his ambition.

Who is here so base that would be a slave? If any, speak — for him have I offended.

Who is here so crude that would not be a Roman? If any, speak — for him have I offended.

Who is here so vile, that will not love his country? If any, speak — for him have I offended.

I pause for a reply.

(*The people are moved by Brutus's words and cheer him.*)

ALL. None, Brutus, none!

BRUTUS. Then none have I offended!
(Antony enters carrying Caesar's body.)

BRUTUS. Here comes his body, mourned by Mark Antony. With these words I depart: As I slew my best friend for the good of Rome, I have the same dagger for myself, when it shall please my country to need my death!

ALL. Live, Brutus! Live, live!

FIRST PERSON. Let him be Caesar!

SECOND PERSON. Caesar's better parts shall be crowned in Brutus!

BRUTUS. Good countrymen, let me depart.
And for my sake, stay here with Antony.
Do grace to Caesar's corpse, and grace his speech
Which Mark Antony, by our permission, is allowed to make.

(*Brutus exits as the people talk among themselves.*)

FIRST PERSON. This Caesar was a tyrant.

THIRD PERSON. That's certain.
We are blest that Rome is rid of him.

(*Antony puts Caesar's body down and goes to the pulpit.*)

SECOND PERSON. Quiet! Let us hear what Antony can say.

ALL. Peace, ho! Let us hear him.

ANTONY. Friends, Romans, countrymen, lend me your ears;
I come to bury Caesar, not to praise him.
The evil that men do lives after them,
The good is oft interred with their bones.
So let it be with Caesar.

The noble Brutus
Hath told you Caesar was ambitious.
If it were so, it was a grievous fault,
And grievously hath Caesar paid for it.
Here, under leave of Brutus and the rest
(For Brutus is an honorable man,
So are they all, all honorable men),
Come I to speak in Caesar's funeral.

He was my friend, faithful and just to me;

But Brutus says he was ambitious,
And Brutus is an honorable man.
He hath brought many captives home to Rome,
Whose ransoms did the royal treasury fill.
Did this in Caesar seem ambitious?
When the poor have cried, Caesar hath wept;
Ambition should be made of sterner stuff.
Yet Brutus says he was ambitious;
And Brutus is an honorable man.

You all did see that
I thrice presented him a kingly crown,
Which he did thrice refuse. Was this ambition?
Yet Brutus says he was ambitious;
And sure he is an honorable man.

I speak not to disprove what Brutus spoke,
But here I am to speak what I do know.

You all did love him once, not without cause;
What cause withholds you then to mourn for him?

(*Antony turns away from the crowd. His grief makes it impossible for him to speak for a moment.*)

ANTONY. Bear with me;
My heart is in the coffin there with Caesar,
And I must pause till it come back to me.

FIRST PERSON. Methinks there is much reason in his sayings.

SECOND PERSON. If thou consider rightly of the matter,
Caesar has had great wrong.

ANTONY. But yesterday the word of Caesar might
Have stood against the world; now lies he there.
O masters! If I were disposed to stir
Your hearts and minds to mutiny and rage
I should do Brutus wrong and Cassius wrong,
Who, you all know, are honorable men.
I will not do them wrong; I rather choose
To wrong the dead, to wrong myself and you,

Than I will wrong such honorable men.

But here's a paper with the seal of Caesar. 'Tis his will.
If people heard this testament —
Which pardon me, I do not mean to read —
They would go and kiss dead Caesar's wounds,
And dip their handkerchiefs in his sacred blood.
Yea, beg a hair of him for memory.

FOURTH PERSON. We'll hear the will. Read it, Mark Antony!

ALL. The will, the will! We will hear Caesar's will!

ANTONY. Have patience, gentle friends, I must not read it.
It is not right you know how Caesar loved you.
You are not wood, you are not stones, but men.
And being men, hearing the will of Caesar,
It will inflame you, it will make you mad.
'Tis good you know not that you are his heirs;
For if you should, O, what would come of it?

FOURTH PERSON. Read the will! We'll hear it, Antony!
You shall read us the will, Caesar's will!

(*Antony's words have succeeded in making the people turn against Brutus and the others.*)

FOURTH PERSON. They were traitors! Not honorable men!

SECOND PERSON. They were villains, murderers! Read the will!

ANTONY. You will force me then to read the will?
Then make a ring about the corpse of Caesar.
And let me show you him that made the will.

(*The people gather around Antony and Caesar's corpse. Antony picks up Caesar's cloak and shows it to the people.*)

ANTONY. If you have tears, prepare to shed them now.
You all do know this cloak.

Look, in this place ran Cassius's dagger through.
See what a tear the envious Casca made.
Through this, the well-beloved Brutus stabbed,
And as he plucked his cursed steel away,
Notice how the blood of Caesar followed it.

Judge, O ye gods, how dearly Caesar loved him!

This was the most unkindest cut of all —
For when the noble Caesar saw him stab,
Great Caesar fell.
O, what a fall was there, my countrymen!
Then I, and you, and all of us fell
While bloody treason ruled over us.

FIRST PERSON. O noble Caesar!

SECOND PERSON. O traitors, villains!

THIRD PERSON. We will be revenged!

ALL. Revenge! Seek! Burn! Fire! Kill! Slay!
Let not a traitor live!

ANTONY. Good Friends, sweet friends, let me not stir you up
To such a sudden flood of mutiny.
They that have done this deed are wise and honorable,
And will, no doubt, with reasons answer you.
I come not, friends, to steal away your hearts;
I am no orator, as Brutus is;
But (as you know me all) a plain blunt man
That loved my friend.

ALL. We'll mutiny.

FIRST PERSON. We'll burn the house of Brutus.

THIRD PERSON. Away, then! Come, seek the conspirators!

(*The crowd leaves, taking Caesar's body.*)

ANTONY. Now let the anger work. Mischief, thou art afoot,
Take thou what course thou wilt!

(A servant enters. He serves Octavius — a young noble Roman leader — who has been away from Rome with his army, fighting for Caesar.)

SERVANT. Sir, Octavius has come to Rome.

ANTONY. Where is he?

SERVANT. He is at Caesar's house.

ANTONY. And there will I go to visit him.
Bring me to Octavius!

ACT IV

Some time has passed since the last act. Brutus and Cassius have had to leave Rome in fear of their lives, but they have gathered an army. Antony and Octavius together rule Rome. They have killed anyone who opposed them. A hundred senators have been killed. These two warriors have gathered an army of their own to hunt down Brutus and Cassius and defeat them.

The scene is Brutus's campsite near Sardis. Brutus and Cassius are in Brutus's tent.

BRUTUS. O Cassius, I am sick with many griefs. Portia is dead.

CASSIUS. Ha? Portia?

BRUTUS. She is dead.

CASSIUS. O unbearable and touching loss!
What sickness came upon her?

BRUTUS. No sickness. She could not endure my absence.

She was stricken with grief that Octavius with Antony
Have made themselves so strong. Her mind became sick,
And (her maids gone), she did swallow hot coals.

CASSIUS. And died so?

BRUTUS. Even so.

(But Brutus must forget his personal grief. Word has come that Antony and Octavius have brought their armies near — to Philippi.)

BRUTUS. Well, to our work. What do you think
Of marching to Philippi immediately?

CASSIUS. I do not think it good.

BRUTUS. Your reason?

CASSIUS. 'Tis better that the enemy seek us.
So shall he waste his means, weary his soldiers,
Doing himself harm, while we — lying still —
Are full of rest and defense.

BRUTUS. Good reasons, but I give you better.
The people between Philippi and this ground
Do not support our cause.
The enemy, marching along through them,
By them shall make a fuller number up.
We cut off this advantage
If we do face Antony at Philippi.

Also, the enemy increases every day;
We — at our height — are ready to decline.
There is a tide in the affairs of men
Which, taken at the flood, leads on to fortune.

CASSIUS. Then go on. We'll meet them at Philippi!
Good night.

BRUTUS. Noble, noble, Cassius. Good night and good repose.

ACT V

Scene 1

The scene is on the plains of Philippi. Octavius and Antony have gathered with their army. A messenger arrives with news about Brutus and Cassius and their armies.

MESSENGER. Prepare you, generals!
The enemy comes, their battle flag hung out!

(A drum sounds. Brutus and Cassius enter with their men. They stand some distance from Antony and Octavius — who watch them, but do not move to fight.)

OCTAVIUS. (To Antony) Mark Antony, shall we give sign of battle?

ANTONY. No, the generals would have some words with us.

BRUTUS. (Calling to Octavius and Antony)
Words before blows. Is it so, countrymen?
Good words are better than bad strokes, Octavius.

ANTONY. In your bad strokes, Brutus, you give good words —
Witness the hole you made in Caesar's heart
Crying: "Long live! Hail, Caesar!"
O you flatterers!

OCTAVIUS. Come, Antony. Away!
(To Brutus and Cassius)
Traitors, if you dare fight today, come to the field!

(Octavius, Antony and their men exit to make ready for battle.)

CASSIUS. This is my birthday; on this very day
Was Cassius born. Now, most noble Brutus,
May the gods today stand friendly and

Let us live our days to old age.

But since the affairs of men are strange,
Let's reason. What is the worst that may happen?
If we do lose this battle, then this is
The very last time we shall speak together.

If we lose, are you contented to be led a captive
Through the streets of Rome?

BRUTUS. No, Cassius, no! Think not, thou noble Roman,
That ever Brutus will go bound to Rome.
He bears too great a mind.
But this same day
Must end that work the ides of March began;
And whether we shall meet again, I know not.
Therefore our last farewell take.
Forever, and forever, farewell, Cassius!
If we do meet again, why, we shall smile.
If not, why then this parting was well made.

CASSIUS. Forever, and forever, farewell, Brutus!
If we do meet again, we'll smile indeed.
If not, 'tis true this parting was well made.

BRUTUS. Why then, lead on. O, that a man might know
The end of this day's business before it comes!
But it is enough that the day will end,
And then the end is known. Come, ho! Away!

Scene 2

The scene is the battlefield. In the distance the battle rages on. Cassius enters with his slave Pindarus. Cassius has watched his friends and soldiers die. He knows the battle will be lost, and he cannot face defeat and capture.

CASSIUS. Come hither, Sirrah!
(He hands Pindarus his sword)
Now be a free man, and with this good sword
That ran through Caesar's bowels, find my bosom.
Answer not. Here, take thou the handle,

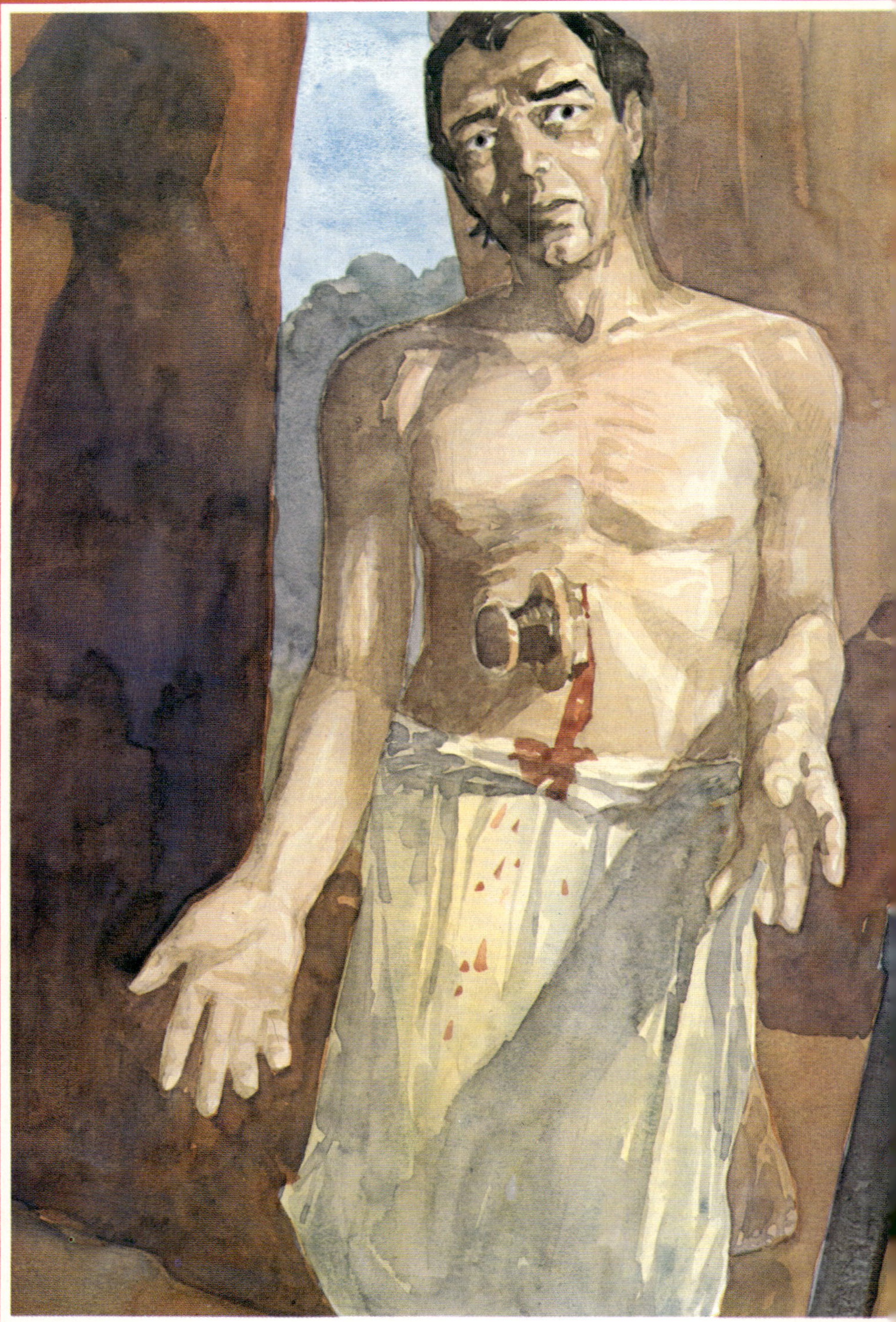

And when my face is covered — as 'tis now —
Guide thou the sword.

(Pindarus holds Cassius's sword, and Cassius pushes himself against it.)

CASSIUS. Caesar, thou art revenged
Even with the sword that killed thee!

(Cassius dies. Pindarus flees away. Cassius's two friends Titinius and Messala enter. They find Cassius dead and run to tell Brutus. He returns with them to Cassius's body.)

BRUTUS. Friends, I owe more tears
To this dead man than you shall see me pay.
I shall find the time, Cassius. I shall find time.

Come, friends, let us to the field!
'Tis three o'clock; and, Romans, before night
We shall try fortune in a second fight!

Scene 3

The scene is another battlefield. The fighting continues, but Brutus's army is nearly completely defeated. Brutus enters with his friends — Volumnius, Clitus, and Strato.

BRUTUS. Our enemies have beat us to the grave.
It is better to leap in ourselves
Than wait till they push us. Good Volumnius,
I prithee, hold my sword while I run on it.

VOLUMNIUS. That's not a task for a friend, my lord.

(The sound of the battle grows closer and closer.)

CLITUS. Fly, fly, my lord. There is no time to wait!

BRUTUS. Farewell to you, my friends. Countrymen,
My heart doth joy that yet in all my life
I found no man but he was true to me.
I shall have more glory by this losing day
Than Octavius and Mark Antony

Shall attain by this evil victory.
So fare you well at once, for Brutus's tongue
Hath ended his life's history.
Night hangs upon mine eyes. My bones would rest.

(*The battle is even closer. Voices cry: "Fly, fly, fly!"*)

CLITUS. Fly, my lord, fly!

BRUTUS. Go! I will follow.

(*All but Brutus and Strato exit.*)

BRUTUS. I prithee, Strato, stay thou by thy lord.
Hold my sword, and turn away thy face,
While I do run upon it. Wilt thou, Strato?

STRATO. Give me your hand first. Fare you well, my lord.

BRUTUS. Farewell, good Strato — Caesar, now be still!
I killed not thee with half so good a will.

(*He runs himself through on the sword Strato holds and dies. Octavius and Antony enter.*)

OCTAVIUS. (To Strato) Where is thy master?

STRATO. Free from bondage,
For Brutus only overcame himself,
And no man else hath honor by his death.

OCTAVIUS. How did your master die?

STRATO. I held the sword, and he did run on it.

(*Antony stands and looks sadly down on Brutus's dead body.*)

ANTONY. This was the noblest Roman of them all.
All the conspirators save only he
Did what they did in envy of great Caesar.
He, only in a general honest thought
And common good to all, made one of them.
His life was gentle, and the elements
So mixed in him that Nature might stand up
And say to all the world: "This was a man!"

GLOSSARY

ambitious (am bish′əs) wanting fame or power

compact (käm′ pakt) an agreement between two or more people

conspirator (kən spir′ ət ər) someone who plans secretly with others to do something wrong

grievous (grē′ vəs) very serious

ides of March (idz əv märch) the fifteenth day of March

inter (in ter′) to put a dead body in the earth or a tomb

petition (pə tish′ ən) a formal, written request made to someone in authority

senate (sen′ ət) a group of people in a government who make the laws

soothsayer (sōōth′ sā′ ər) a person who tells what will happen in the future

superstitious (sōō pər stish′ əs) someone who has beliefs based on fear or ignorance

tyrant (tī′ rənt) a strong ruler who uses his power in a cruel way

valiant (val′ yənt) brave or courageous